From the people who brought you

KenDoku

Volume 1

100 PUZZLES TO BUILD YOUR BRAIN

By David Levy & Robert Fuhrer

Published by Seven Footer Press
276 Fifth Ave., Suite 301
New York, NY 10001

First Printing, February 2009
10 9 8 7 6 5 4 3 2

Kendoku is a trademark of Nextoy, LLC

KenKen is a trademark of Nextoy LLC used under license.
Puzzle contents © Gakken Co. Ltd. All rights reserved.

Design by Junko Miyakoshi

ISBN-13 978-1-934734-14-8

www.sevenfooterpress.com

Introduction

KenDoku™ is a brilliant new puzzle, brought to you by the same people who launched KenKen™.

KenDoku combines the features of KenKen with those of sudoku, creating a perfect marriage of those magnificent number puzzles. **KenDoku** comes in two different grid sizes, 6x6 and 9x9, so everyone can choose the size that best matches the time they want to spend on a puzzle and their own solving skills. Within each grid size the puzzles come in a wide range of levels of difficulty—the easiest ones can be solved by bright children whilst the most difficult ones present a real challenge to even the most experienced solvers. It is this combination of different grid sizes with a range of difficulty levels that makes **KenDoku** a great puzzle for everyone!

As with KenKen, one of the key features of **KenDoku** is the fun that can be had from using logic combined with the simple basic arithmetic skills: addition, subtraction, multiplication and division. This feature also works as a great way to enhance your arithmetic skills, so children (and adults) will be able to improve their mental arithmetic abilities almost subconsciously while they are enjoying the solving process.

The two of us are puzzle enthusiasts who were addicted to sudoku until we came across KenKen and now **KenDoku**, both of which have supplanted sudoku in our affections. We are confident that you will share in our enthusiasm as you try **KenDoku**. This is a puzzle with a truly great future!

David Levy & Bob Fuhrer
December 2008

Hints for Solving KenDoku™ Puzzles

David Levy

There are only two rules of KenDoku and they are very simple.

Rule 1

All of the numbers from 1 up to the grid size (6 or 9) must appear in every row and every column and every block. So in a 6×6 KenDoku puzzle, for example, each of the numbers 1-6 must appear once and only once in every row and every column and every 3×2 block. And in a 9×9 KenDoku puzzle, each of the numbers 1-9 must appear once and only once in every row and every column and every 3×3 block.

Rule 2

The other rule is that in every "cage" enclosed by a thick line, the target number in the top left-hand square of that cage is calculated from the numbers in all the squares in the cage, using the addition, subtraction, multiplication or division operation indicated by the symbol.

Here are examples of both grid sizes where you can see that the above rules have been followed. First a completed 6x6 puzzle. The 3x2 blocks are shown by the dashed lines.

Next is a completed 9x9 puzzle, in which the 3x3 blocks are shown by dashed lines.

35× 7	2÷ 2	4	144× 3	8— 9	1	16+ 6	8	4— 5
5	18+ 9	3 3	8	6	3— 7	4	2	1
2— 6	8	15+ 1	2	4	5	3	2— 7	9
4	1	5	12+ 7	3	144× 6	8	9 9	5— 2
2— 8	6	7— 9	10+ 4	5	1— 2	1	1— 3	7
3÷ 3	3— 7	2	1	1— 8	9	5 5	4	3— 6
9	4	11+ 6	5	7 7	21+ 8	2÷ 2	1	3
5+ 2	3	15+ 7	6× 6	1	4	9	3— 5	8
4— 1	5	8	9 9	6× 2	3	17+ 7	6	4

Solving KenDoku puzzles requires a mixture of logic and simple arithmetic. The logical process makes use of the information you have as to what numbers are, or could be, in which squares of the grid. Arithmetic enables you to narrow down the possibilities. You will probably find it helpful to pencil possible numbers (we call them "candidates") into a square and then eliminate candidates as more numbers become known.

We start by explaining the most important simple methods employed in solving KenDoku puzzles.

"Unused" Numbers in a Row or Column

Take a look at this row from a 6×6 KenDoku puzzle.

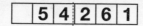

We can see that five of the squares have already been solved, with the numbers 1, 2, 4, 5, and 6. One of the numbers from 1-6 is currently "unused" in this row, and that is 3. There is only one empty square in the row and so we can deduce that it must contain a 3.

Now look at this row.

Here we can see that only four of the squares have been filled in, with the numbers 1, 2, 4, and 6. The other two squares, which we have labelled A and B, have no numbers in them yet. The numbers 3 and 5 are currently unused in this row. We know that 3 and 5 must both be in this row, because every number from 1 to 6 must be in this row, so we can be sure that one of A and B is 3 and the other is 5. We do not yet know which is which, so it would be helpful to use a pencil to write both 3 and 5 in square A, and both 3 and 5 in square B, until there is enough information to decide which is which.

"Unused" Numbers in a Block

Here are two blocks from a 6x6 KenDoku puzzle.

On the left of this diagram is an almost completed block (3 squares by 2). We can see that the numbers for five of the six squares in this block have already been identified: 1, 2, 3, 4, and 6. The only square remaining in this block to be filled is square G, so G must be 5 because it is the only unused number in this block.

Note that we now have quite a lot of information that can be helpful in solving the block on the right-hand side of the diagram: DEF KLM. We know that none of D, E, and F can be 1, 2, or 6, because these numbers are all in the same row, and that none of K, L, and M can be 3, 4, or 5 because those numbers are all in the same row.

Only One Number in a Cage is Missing

Since we know the total for every cage, if we find a cage that has only one missing number we can often calculate that number by knowing the total and the other numbers in the cage.

Here is an example of a cage with three squares. The total in this cage is 12, and is created by addition. We already have two of the three numbers in the cage: 3 and 5. These two numbers add up to 8, so the empty square must contain 4 in order for the total to be 12.

A similar approach will always work for cages with multiplication—there will be only one number that can possibly go in the empty square. But where the symbol is subtraction or division we might not be certain which of two numbers it could be, as in the next example.

Here we wish to calculate A. It could be 6 (6-4 = 2) or it could be 2 (4-2 = 2). Remember that the subtraction symbol means that the total is the difference between the two numbers in the cage, it does not indicate which square contains the larger of the two numbers.

Similarly, the division symbol means that the total is created by dividing one of the numbers in the cage by the other, but it does not indicate which of the squares in that cage contains the larger of the two numbers.

Only One Set of Numbers Can Make the Correct Total
Sometimes we will find a cage for which there is only one set of numbers that can possibly make the correct total.

Here we have a cage of two numbers that add up to 4. The only possible ways to make a total of 4 using two numbers are 2+2 or 1+3. But A and B cannot both be 2 because we cannot have the same number more than once in any row, in any column, or in any block. So the two numbers must be 1 and 3. We do not yet know which is which, so it would be helpful to use a pencil to write both 1 and 3 in square A, and both 1 and 3 in square B, until we have enough information to decide which is which.

Here is another example of this method.

In this case we have a cage of two numbers that we know multiply to make 10. The only way we can do this in any KenDoku puzzle, using two numbers, is with 2 and 5. So we know that one of A and B is 2 and the other is 5. We do not yet know which is which, so it would be helpful to use a pencil to write both 2 and 5 in squares A and B until we can decide which is which.

The Only Possible Solution to a Cage that Covers More than One Row or Column

Sometimes we will come across a cage that has only one possible way to make the given total with however many numbers we are allowed to use, and it is also possible for us to decide exactly which numbers go in which squares of that cage.

The most commonly seen example of this is an "L" shaped cage with three squares.

Here we have a cage of three squares in which the total, created by addition, is 4. It is easy to see that the only three numbers that add up to 4 are 1, 1, and 2. But we cannot have two number 1s in the same row (the upper row here), and we cannot have two number 1s in the same column (the left column here). So the only way to arrange 1, 1, and 2 that complies with the rules is for A to be 2 and for B and C both to be 1. In this example, in one fell swoop, we have not only worked out what the three numbers must be, we have also worked out exactly which squares have which numbers. You will not always be this fortunate, but you will often be able to decide exactly what set of numbers must go in a cage.

Solving a KenDoku Puzzle Step-by-Step

Now we are going to solve a whole 6×6 KenDoku puzzle step-by-step. The same methods used in this example can be employed for solving 9×9 KenDoku puzzles. Follow this example carefully and you will become familiar with the most important methods for solving KenDoku.

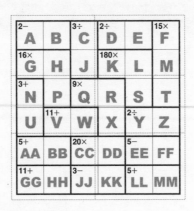

Step 1   Discovering the certainties

The best way to start a KenDoku puzzle is always to look for cages where we can be absolutely certain what the numbers are. Sometimes we are given one or more single square cages—in these cages the "total" shown in the top left corner of the square is the number that goes into that square, so we can write it in at once.

Here we can see that the FMT cage contains three numbers that multiply together to make a total of 15. The only three numbers that can go in this cage are 1, 3, and 5, so we can pencil in all three of those candidate numbers in each of the three squares: F, M, and T.

The KLS cage contains three numbers that multiply together to make a total of 180. One of these numbers must be a 5, because any KenDoku total ending in 5 or 0 can only be made by multiplication if at least one of the numbers in that cage is a 5. And if one of the numbers in the KLS cage is a 5, the other two numbers must multiply together to make 36, because $5 \times 36 = 180$. The only two numbers from 1 to 6 that multiply together to make 36 are 6×6, so two of the numbers in the KLS cage must be 6s. But we cannot have more than one 6 in any row or any column, so the only possible arrangement of a 5 and two 6s in this cage is for K and S to be 6 and for L to be 5.

The NU cage has two numbers adding up to 3. The only way for this to be possible is for one of N and U to be 1 and the other to be 2. We do not yet know which is which, so we should pencil both 1 and 2 into both squares: N and U.

The QRX cage has three numbers that multiply together to make 9. This is only possible with numbers from 1 to 6 if two of these numbers are 3 and the other is 1. But we cannot have more than one 3 in any row or any column, so the only possible arrangement of a 1 and two 3s is for Q and X to be 3 and for R to be 1.

The VW cage has two numbers adding up to 11. The only way for this to be possible with numbers from 1 to 6 is for one of V and W to be 5 and the other to be 6. We do not yet know which is which, so we should pencil both 5 and 6 into both squares: V and W.

The CC DD cage has two numbers that multiply to make 20. The only way for this to be possible with numbers from 1 to 6 is for one of CC and DD to be 4 and the other to be 5. We do not yet know which is which, so we should pencil both 4 and 5 into both squares: CC and DD.

The EE FF cage has two numbers with a difference of 5. The only way for this to be possible with numbers from 1 to 6 is for one of EE and FF to be 1 and the other to be 6. We know that EE cannot be 6 because there is already a 6 in that column (in S), so EE must be 1 and FF must therefore be 6.

The GG HH cage is just like the VW cage. There are two numbers adding up to 11, and the only way for this to be possible with numbers from 1 to 6 is for one of GG and HH to be 5 and the other to be 6. We do not yet know which is which, so we should pencil both 5 and 6 into both squares: GG and HH.

We have now found all of the more obvious certainties, and the grid with our pencil markings looks like this:

2− A	B	3÷ C	2÷ D	E	15× 135
16× G	H	J	180× 6	5	135
3+ 12	P	9× 3	1	6	135
12	11+ 56	56	3	2÷ Y	Z
5+ AA	20× BB	45	45	5− 1	6
11+ 56	56	3− JJ	KK	5+ LL	MM

Step 2   Making simple logical deductions from what we know already

We can now use what we know already to eliminate certain possibilities, and thereby to discover new information.

Earlier we could see that square N must be 1 or 2, but we did not know which. Now that we know that R is 1 we can be certain that N is 2, since they are both in the same row, and this means that U must be 1. So we can delete one of the candidates from each of the squares: N and U, leaving 2 as the only number in N and 1 as the only number in U.

We know that the NPQ UVW block must contain each of the numbers from 1 to 6. We can see that the numbers 1, 2, and 3 are already placed, and we know that V and W use up the 5 and 6 in this block, so the only remaining square in this block, square P, must be taken by the only remaining number for this block, which is 4.

Now that N, P, Q, R, and S are all known, we can eliminate the 1 and 3 as candidates for T and we therefore know that T must be 5. This knowledge allows us to eliminate 5 as a candidate in both F and M.

CC, DD, EE, and FF take care of 1, 4, 5, and 6, so the two remaining numbers in that row, AA and BB, must be 2 and 3. But AA cannot be 2 because there is already a 2 in that column (in square N), so AA must be 3 and BB is 2.

Let us now see how the grid looks.

2− A	B	3÷ C	2÷ D	E	15× 13
16× G	H	J	180× 6	5	13
3+ 2	4	9× 3	1	6	5
1	11+ 56	56	3	2÷ Y	Z
5+ 3	2	20× 45	45	5− 1	6
11+ 56	56	3− JJ	KK	5+ LL	MM

Step 3   Making more deductions from what we now know

The GHP cage has three numbers that multiply together to make 16, but we already know that P is 4. So G × H must be 4, which means that both G and H must be 2 or one of them must be 4 and the other 1. Since we cannot have two 2s in the same row we know that both G and H cannot be 2, and since H cannot be 4 because of the 4 in the same column (P) we can be certain that G is 4 and H is 1.

Because of the 1 in H we can eliminate 1 as a candidate for M, which means that M must be 3 and F must be 1.

With five out of the six possible numbers in the second row already known, we can be certain that J is 2.

Since J is 2 we know that C must be 6 since C ÷ 2 = 3. (Clearly there is no way for 2 ÷ C to be 3.)

Since C is 6 we know that W cannot be 6 so W must be 5.

Since W is 5 we know that V must be 6, and CC cannot be 5 so CC must be 4. Since CC is 4 we know that DD must be 5.

Since V is 6 we know that HH must be 5 and GG must therefore be 6.

With five out of the six numbers in the first (leftmost) column already known, we can be certain that A is 5 (the only unused number in that column).

With five out of the six numbers in the second column already known, we can be certain that B is 3 (the only unused number in that column). We can verify this because the difference between 5 and 3 is 2, corresponding to the 2- total in square A.

With five out of the six numbers in the third column already known, we can be certain that JJ is 1 (the only unused number in that column); and since JJ is 1 we know that KK must be 4 because the difference between JJ and KK is 3.

With five out of the six numbers in the fourth column already known, we can be certain that D is 2 (the only unused number in that column).

With five out of the six numbers in the top row now known, we can be certain that E is 4 (the only unused number in that row).

If we look at the current state of the grid we can see that only four numbers remain to be discovered.

Final step   The rest is easy

If we look along the row from U to Z we can see that 1, 3, 5, and 6 are already used, so Y must be 2 or 4 and Z must be 2 or 4. But if we look in the column containing Y, we can see that 4 is already used (in square E), so Y cannot be 4. This means that Y must be 2 and Z is therefore 4.

Now the two rightmost columns each have five numbers, so LL is the only unused number in the fifth column, which is 3, and MM is the only unused number in the sixth column, which is 2. We can verify this because 3 + 2 = 5, which is the total for the LL MM cage.

We have now solved the whole puzzle! Here is the completed solution grid.

2− **5**	**3**	3÷ **6**	2÷ **2**	**4**	15× **1**
16× **4**	**1**	**2**	180× **6**	**5**	**3**
3+ **2**	**4**	9× **3**	**1**	**6**	**5**
1	11+ **6**	**5**	**3**	2÷ **2**	**4**
5+ **3**	**2**	20× **4**	**5**	5− **1**	**6**
11+ **6**	**5**	3− **1**	**4**	5+ **3**	**2**

These reasoning methods will enable you to solve Easy KenDoku puzzles and will help you make progress in solving more difficult ones.

A Very Useful Trick

As you progress to the more difficult 6x6 KenDoku puzzles and to the 9 × 9 puzzles, you will find that there are other tricks that help you make certain types of deductions. Here is the most common of the slightly more advanced tricks. If you learn this, you will find that many of the 9 × 9 KenDoku puzzles (and some of the more difficult 6x6 puzzles) will become easier for you to solve.

Take a look at this row from a 9 × 9 puzzle on which the solving process has already started and some possible numbers have been pencilled in. (We call possible numbers "candidates.") We can see that there are three squares that contain, in various combinations, the candidates 1, 2, and 3.

Since we have three squares and three numbers for those squares, we can be certain that one of these numbers must be in one of the three squares, another of the three numbers must be in another of the three squares, and the third number must be in the remaining one of these three squares. It is therefore impossible for any of the other squares in this row (B, C, E, F, H, or J) to contain any of the numbers 1, 2, or 3. If any of the numbers 1, 2, or 3 are already pencilled in to any of those squares (B, C, E, F, H, or J) then we can safely delete them. During the remainder of the solution process we should take care to avoid pencilling in 1, 2, or 3 as candidates for any of the currently empty squares in this row.

This same trick works for blocks as well as for rows and columns. The same trick also works just as well for combinations of two numbers spread across exactly two squares in a row, column or block, and for combinations of four numbers spread across exactly four squares, etc. When you try solving 9×9 puzzles you will soon realize how helpful this trick can be in eliminating certain possibilities.

Good Luck!

Now that you have learned the most important strategies for tackling KenDoku puzzles you are in good shape to start solving. We suggest that you begin with the Easy puzzles with 6x6 grids, and as you develop your KenDoku skills move on to the Medium and Difficult 6x6 puzzles.

You will probably be ready to try the Easy 9x9 puzzles even before you have solved all of the 6x6 puzzles. This is because "Easy" refers to the strategies needed to solve a puzzle, not to the amount of time needed to solve it. Puzzles designated Easy do not need you to employ any strategies more advanced than those you have already learned in this tutorial section, so when you move on to Easy 9x9 puzzles, you will find that the solving techniques are not advanced, it simply takes longer to solve a 9x9 Easy puzzle because of the increased number of squares and cages.

So you are now ready to begin. Good luck, and happy KenDoku-ing!

2÷		7+		3	9+
2×	2−		3÷		
		7+	20×		3÷
11+			3÷		
8+	2÷		11+		1
	5−		4	1−	

15×		5+		3÷	
32×		11+	15×		3+
5−			14+		
	3÷	2÷		5−	1−
5			8×		
11+					5

5−	40×		24×	3÷	
	2÷			20×	3+
40×		15×			
			10+	2	24×
6+				14+	
4		5−			

11+	2÷	2÷		3−	1−
		2÷	4−		
3−	14+			2÷	
		3÷		2×	3
6×		4−	1−		
	4			30×	

3−	36×			60×	
	3−		5−		
30×	1	10+	15×		5−
	1−		2÷		
		2÷	11+		2
11+			3	3−	

3÷		2	40×	11+	
13+				4−	3÷
	12+				
3−	5−		15×	24×	
	120×				3÷
		3÷		4	

5−	12+	3÷		12×	
			3−		
6×			2÷	5−	90×
80×		6			
	180×	3×		1−	
					2

2÷		1	120×	6×	4−
5−	15×				
	2−			5−	1−
8+	432×		7+		
	5				4−
3+			2−		

60×			3÷		1
11+		3÷		20×	11+
	12×	2÷			
11+		3÷		1−	
		5	80×	5−	5+
2÷					

1−	16+		2−		3
			5×		3−
24×		11+		36×	
5×			3		24×
		5+	2÷		
10+				4−	

6+			4	1−	
15+			2×		2÷
2÷	15×			11+	
	2÷	5−	2÷		
20×				1−	5+
	6	2−			

3−		60×	3+		4
4×			10+	11+	11+
	30×				
120×					9×
	4	4−			
	3÷		11+		

13

6×6 EASY

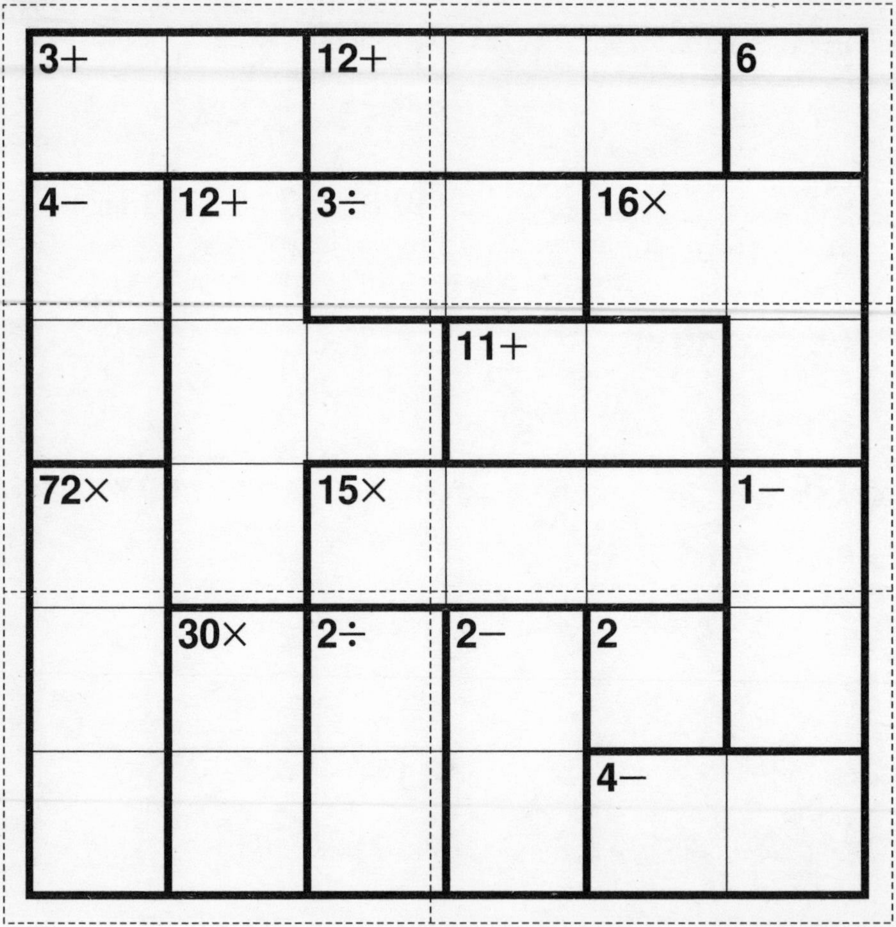

4	3+		60×		72×
11+		36×	5×		
2÷					
	14+			2÷	
2−		9+		3÷	
3÷			2−		5

2÷		4	10×		
3÷	5	2−		2÷	
	10×		1−	3+	1−
2÷	5−				
	15+	3÷	2÷		6+
			2÷		

14+		16×	3−		10+
	2				
6×		5−		20×	
6×	20×		2−	3÷	2÷
		5+			
1−			6	3÷	

11+		2	6×	2−	15×
2÷	3÷				
		2÷		5	2−
18×	20×		3+		
	30×	13+		3÷	
				3÷	

2÷	20×	11+		1−	
		180×		1	1−
1−			5−		
	108×	3+	40×		
			1−	4−	
4−		4		3÷	

17+		2×	6	24×	
	3				25×
	13+				
2−	9+		3÷		7+
	3÷		6+		
5+		2−		4−	

2÷		4−	2÷		3−
1−	3÷		10+		
		7+			5
25×		3−		2÷	
	24×			20×	2÷
6	3+				

3	2÷		540×		6+
30×			5+		
1−	9+				
	2÷		3−	2÷	
12×		9+		5−	
3÷				1−	

22

4−		16×		60×	3÷
8+					
2	120×	90×	3÷	40×	
				6	
1−			6×		2−
	10×				

4	13+	6×		1−	6×
1−			3×		
	2÷	20×			24×
6+			3−		
	24×		3÷		
5−			60×		

10+		4	1−		10+
	48×		25×		
		2÷			8×
2	2−		2−		
72×		10×		30×	
			5−		

16+		2÷		3−	
		3	120×	2−	
11+				9+	
	5×		2÷		
8+	12+		4	11+	
			6×		

3−	14+	40×			6
			5−	2÷	3÷
2	2−				
11+	2÷	5−	1−	2−	
				3−	
12×			60×		

3	3+	1−	11+		9+
3÷			3×	1−	
	720×				
5+		3	9+		
			1−		1−
2−		7+			

2−		9+	1−		90×
8+			5−	2÷	
	4				
36×			4	6+	
2−	2÷	13+		3÷	
			4−		4

45

1−	5−	5	2÷		11+
		2÷		5−	
5−	40×	15×			
			1−	2−	5−
9+	1−	7+			
			9+		

2÷		5−		30×	
1−	6×	15+			
			2÷	1−	
20×	3	2÷		6×	
			10×		2−
90×				1	

3÷		20×	12+		
12×			5−		2÷
	30×		1−		
4−	8+	3÷		2÷	1−
			8+		
6	1−			5+	

12+			30×	12×	2
4−					
5−	10+	2÷		1−	
			16×		3−
2−	2÷			5	
	2−		6×		

3−	4−	24×			12+
		2	180×	12+	
4−	4				
	1−		3÷		3÷
11+					
1−		1−		5−	

34

11+		3+		1−	
2÷		2÷		4−	
1−	24×		3÷		1−
		60×	1−	1−	
15×	4				2÷
			5−		

11+	24×			2÷	60×
	9+	3−			
3÷			2÷		
	1−		1−	1−	2
9+		3−			7+
2÷			9+		

12×		7+		3+	2−
5−	1−	3÷			
		10+		1−	3÷
7+	2÷	18×			
				14+	
3÷		11+			

3÷	4	9+	4−		13+
			10+		
5−		2÷			
11+	5+		36×	5+	
				10+	
2−		120×			

9+	2−		2−		15×
		120×			
1−	5−		5+	4	
	5			2−	2−
6+	2÷	12+			
			6	1−	

11+	2−		2÷		1−
		15+			
	1−			4−	
15+	3×	13+		3÷	2÷
	12×			1−	

3÷		1−	1−		10+
2÷			2÷	7+	
1−	5−	6×			
			72×		
11+		6+		11+	
	1−		1−		

6×		5	2−		2−
	2−	1−	2÷		
1−			5−		2÷
	2÷		2−		
4−		2÷		10+	
7+		1−		2	

9+		120×			1
	48×		10+		
12+			18×		
		15+		2÷	
2−				1−	3÷
2÷		12×			

30×		11+	10+	1−	2
					9+
6+	3÷	3			
		1−		1−	
10+	6×	13+		4−	1−

12+		10+			4
60×		2÷		6×	
		6×	11+	2	
12+				16+	
	2−	16+			
				1−	

30×	1	1−		8+	
	15+		2÷		
5+			1−	5−	1−
	12+	2÷			
			6+	2÷	3−
13+					

4−		48×		90×	
5+			12×		
14+				13+	
12×			1−		96×
7+	3−				
	6	3÷			

15+			30×		
1−		15+		5+	2÷
24×	8+				
			1−	3−	
		12×		1−	2÷
7+					

2÷		5	36×	12+	
3÷					16+
180×		4×			
			12+		1−
1−	5−	1−			
			12+		

1−		24×			7+
16+		2−		2÷	
		30×			1−
3÷	2÷			19+	
	120×	2			
		1−		6+	

4	1−		6×		
6+			60×	1−	
10+		8×			13+
10+				2÷	
	6	4−			
	1−		12×		

2÷	5	567×		2−		7−	7+	
	1−	42×		2−			30×	
4−			40×	3×		3÷	63×	
	12+				84×		5	21×
420×		2÷				8−		
		4×	135×		13+		4÷	3÷
56×					105×			
3	1−		3÷	2÷			8−	
8−		2		4−		17+		

2÷		14+	15+	3−	9×		252×	7−
2−								
27×			1−		36×	4×	11+	
5−	1−	2−		8×				1−
		2÷			5	180×	17+	
3+		16+	7+	18+				7
40×					14×	18+	45×	
4	6×		5×					
15+				2÷		7	1−	

18+		4÷		1512×		7×	60×	
2÷		25×						6−
	1−			36×	2−		63×	
15×		6−				18+		8−
	4	14×		8−	60×			
8+	3+	192×					2	90×
			5−	12+		17+		
1−		10+		4÷	8+		28×	
30×			4		7−			

84×		432×	14+		2÷		5−	
3+			21×	5−		240×		
	11+			2÷	5−		81×	140×
4		5−	3÷					
15×	17+			4−	15+		12+	
		9×			2−			
23+	3−			1−	6	11+		240×
	8+	12×	4−		8−			
				2−		3	7−	

17+	90×		8−	56×		6×		5+
	7			240×		1−		
3+		3−			135×	15+		17+
3−	5−		2÷			2÷		
		24+		17+		2÷	8−	7
12×				4×				60×
42×	4−	30×				3÷		
			72×		12+		12+	
3	8−		3÷			3−		

40×		270×	2÷		16+			4÷
3÷	28×			72×		9+		
		2÷	1−		14+		7−	17+
10+			35×			56×		
5−	17+	72×		2−			6+	2÷
			15+		2	16×		
432×	3+	7		11+				2−
		12+	2÷	16+	2−		6	
					8−		6−	

3+	3÷		28×		3÷	8−	13+	
	56×		2−				3÷	12×
1−		17+		8−		140×		
17+	3+			2−				13+
	2÷	11+		2÷	90×			
84×		16+			12+	14+	3×	
	5−	9						1−
		6×		20+			4	
240×				5−		10+		2

28×	2−	3÷		3+	15×	1−	17+	35×
		9	28×					
9×		13+		17+		3÷		
			3÷		13+	1−	6+	2−
80×	17+		2−					
	14+		1−		8−		5+	
	5		8−	5−	60×	126×		
15+	2÷	105×					15+	
				28×			6	

2−	5−	8+		8−		21+		
		4÷		4	8+		8−	
9×		2÷		1−		3−		2−
216×		2	40×		126×	1−	1−	
	140×	6×						3
			7+		2÷	2×		11+
5	4−		3−			42×		
5−	2÷	8−	56×	6+	2÷		160×	
						3÷		

11+		42×			2÷		17+	10+
3+	1−	15+		8−	175×	7		
		2÷					14×	
10+	4÷		1−	90×				45×
	12+			10+	4×			
15+		8−				7+		336×
	2÷	20×		11+		17+		
8		4−		1−	11+		60×	
2−		2÷						2

2÷		8×			17+		5−	120×
8−		4÷	18+	35×		96×		
35×							4÷	
10×		24×		120×	8−			19+
2−		7			14×	3÷		
13+		18×		2			3−	
2÷			63×			105×		3+
4−	8−		4÷	1−			2−	
	10×			15+				9

3−		56×		8−		13+		
189×	15+		13+	7+		1	7+	
	4÷			6	3÷	40×	8−	4−
	15+		2÷					
15+	2÷	9×		14+		1−	5−	
			2−				5−	2÷
	35×		6	17+		2−		
7−	3÷	3÷		2−			1−	
		3+		252×			11+	

84×			3+		315×	60×	5−	36×
3+		17+						
432×	15+			4÷	5−		784×	
	9		210×					
	210×	2			4÷		24+	
		7×	9	4÷		12×		
			4÷	18+			16+	
2−	24×				49×	8−		
	1−		1−				3÷	

30+		2÷		36×		11+		11+
		4÷	15+	2−		2÷	8−	
15×				3÷				7
19+				1344×	25×		6−	
9+		17+					6	13+
	14+				64×			
36×		5	2÷			14×		
4−	120×			8−	2−		2÷	11+
	28×				1−			

5−	72×		3÷		17+	3÷	6+	13+
		20+						
8−	25×		4−		96×	17+	10+	
	2		84×				120×	
17+				1−	6−		5−	
3	14+		8−		5−			15+
160×				11+		5		
	8−		2÷	2÷	35×	48×		
84×						36×		

3+	2÷		3−		64×	315×		36×
	140×	72×	2−					
			15+		2÷		1	
17+	3÷		2	12+			144×	6−
		14+	21+					
2−			64×		6	5−	36×	
	3+		8−		140×		60×	
2−	13+			36×		3÷		288×
	63×							

1−	17+	1−		18×	3−		4÷	
		140×			20×		10+	
5×			7+	9	17+	2÷		17+
				1−		6−		
6	189×		16×		90×		15×	
17+			12+				15+	
	15+	64×	7		9×			
						16+		17+
9+		3÷		11+		1		

20×			14+	3−	3÷		7	5−
378×					16×		60×	
42×	17+	9×		2−				
		11+		2−	64×		3−	
	6					10+	20+	
192×	3+		7	14+				
		15+	5−	30×			17+	6−
15×				5−		2		
3+		22+			1−		1−	

15+	180×		17+	2	9×	13+		11+
				1−				
3×		5−	11+		14+	5−		7−
20+						14+		
		4−		17+		14+	21×	
19+	8	3+		2÷			1−	
	2÷	189×			56×			1−
		25×	24×			108×		
6−					2		15+	

2÷		14+		11+		3+		24+
8	108×			3+		11+		
5−	11+	36×		200×		28×	9×	
			17+	8				
3÷	12+	2÷			81×		6−	
		1−				1−		24×
23+		2	12+			1−		
1−		21×	9+	63×		3÷		
				11+			4−	

90×			5−		8×	9+		960×
252×		3+	8+					
	8		5−	2÷	2÷		27+	
15×	10+				4−			
		17+	2÷	3−	13+			
9+					168×		8−	
17+	2÷	6+		3÷			9+	
		3−		1−	13+		540×	
5−		24×			2			

13+	18+		26+	3+		13+		
				140×		17+		6−
	14+					5	10×	
20×	16+		48×			3−		
	2÷	21×			6		21+	
17+		1−	1−		3÷			
	160×		4−		6×		2−	
2÷		12+		49×		20×		3÷
		8−		4÷				

14+		36×	4÷	4	3−		63×	
				14+		27×	9+	4÷
18+		6−		3−				
	3+	240×	140×		17+		24×	1−
3÷								
	14+		6	8+			3−	
		21×		90×			2÷	
20×		8−		672×	5−		2÷	
5−					20×		8−	

6+	1−	9+	2−		2÷		54×	
			54×			120×	2÷	
15+			1−				49×	
20×		6−	11+	17+	2÷	48×		
6×						8−		90×
336×		4−		3×	5−	2÷	14+	
	3−							
18×		8	24×		63×			24×
	17+			2−				

20×	3÷	20+			3+		13+	21+
		14+			5−	3÷		
8−		1−		2÷			8+	
11+		4×			9	168×		5−
672×			5	13+			7−	
		45×	6−		12+	1−		36×
2÷	1−							
		72×		3÷		126×		5
21×			18+			8		

432×			30+	6+			140×	
12×					336×		27×	
4−	10+					24+		
		8	9×	18+			2÷	3÷
9+					2160×			
14+	4−	4÷					6+	3÷
		1−				12×		
	4−		108×	6	5×		23+	
64×								

6	4−		6−		20+			36×
5−		18+	35×		8−		20×	
2÷			9×	5−		2−		
	18+	15+			10+		8−	3−
8−			23+					
				4	98×		3−	
2−	2÷	17+	2	20+	8×		5−	
						4	3÷	8−
15+		10+			2−			

24+			2÷		22+		2−	2−
40×	5−		4	18+				
					13+		16+	4÷
16+	5−		45×	14+	9×			
	4÷						2−	
	45×		5−		10+		17+	
4÷	15×			21×	18+	19+	7	30×
		13+	48×					
4÷							1−	

120×			3+		1008×	19+		7
2−		8−	4−					5+
14+			2÷			10×		
	72×		7	1−	8−		13+	
4÷		5−				3÷		4÷
	17+	3−		3÷	160×	1−	28×	
21+		18×						108×
	4÷		2−			10+		
		378×					8×	

7	288×		2÷		19+		5−	
8−		20×	18+				96×	
			2÷	4÷	17+			7−
10×		24+				5−		
2÷				30×		24×	3−	84×
	5−		6−					
18+			8−		1344×	2÷	28+	
1−		2÷						
17+			2−		56×			

1−		17+	9+		1−	23+		7+
19+			11+	1−				
	3−	3−			35×		8−	
			2÷		9×		3−	
2÷		1−		4−			42×	
2÷	19+			24+	4÷		36×	
	10+				8+		5−	
16+	24×	35×			2−	4÷		3÷
			2÷			14+		

18+	448×		13+			8−		48×
				7	27+			
	8−	180×	1−	7−		3−		
				17+	2÷		1−	
1−			4−			3+		19+
36×				1008×				
3÷		3÷	1−			13+		8−
140×			4÷		15×	1−		
1		72×				84×		

105×		15+				5	1512×	
2−		7+		2	8−			48×
	24+	4−	210×			4÷		
1−			8−	10+				
		54×		4−	3−	1−	9	210×
3−			3÷					
45×	2÷			1−		2−	5+	10+
	2÷		29+	11+				
1−					144×			

22+		70×			2÷		14+	6−
	2−		14+		7−			
	7	13+	16×			8−	1−	3÷
3−			8+		22+			
72×	18+			2		120×		
			23+				49×	9+
	7−			2÷				
1−		2÷		10+		3÷		4−
30×		19+				2÷		

64×	16+			3−		1−		3÷
	14+	4×		2−		3÷		
		14+		2−		17+		4−
2−	5−			14×	3×			
			144×		13+		19+	4÷
108×		4−						
			5−	24×		40×		3−
3÷	192×				2−		9	
		24+				2÷		6

14+		5×	1−		16+	17+		336×
4−								
	1−		36×	7−	4	9+		
4−		28×			1−	8	18×	
9	48×		3−			18+		16+
14+		17+		16+				
	4÷		30×		2÷		140×	17+
					3+			
5−		5−		14+				6

4÷	2−	2÷		7−	3024×		11+	
		3−					15+	6−
17+		13+		2−		14+		
2÷		80×	2−					270×
2−				12+	2×		56×	
21+	14+		1−					
		8×			1−		2÷	
	20+			3÷		5−	9+	
			13+				8×	

3−		14+		8	2÷	3÷		15+
4−		24×		2−		7+		
3÷			16+		2÷		13+	28×
4−	15+			60×		24+		
							36×	
4	19+			7×		15+		
80×	2÷	84×		60×				8−
		9				3−		
	12+			1−		90×		

3÷		12+		3−		1−	4÷	
3+	17+		17+	10+			17+	
		36×			2÷		1−	
4−			1−		1−			15+
	2÷	5−		1−		2−	7	
42×		1−		1	3÷		10×	
	4−		14+			17+		1−
2÷	42×			54×		6−		
		8−		3−		3÷		3

560×		336×		3÷		29+		
				25+				5−
3−					14+	1−		
2−		504×		3+			9	2−
30×					16+	2÷		
	3×	4032×		33+		15+		
					4−		1−	
4					7−		42×	3−
17+		6+		2÷				

1−		49×		2−	14+		15+	2÷
1−			4−					
1−	11+			1−		14+		1−
		9+		3−			11+	
3−	5−	24×		162×		2÷		
		72×		25×				84×
8−	1−		11+			26+		
				1−			18+	
2−		6	2÷					

48×		18+	1080×		10+		2÷	
					1−	1−	45×	15+
108×	10+		1−					
		17+			56×			1−
5	14×	14+		6−		3−		
56×			54×		16+		3−	
				2−			3	23+
3−	3−		13+	35×		18+		
	2−						4÷	

2	1−		18+	20×		3÷		14+
8−	1−				4−	3−	252×	
	11+		17+					
8×		14+			9	30+	2÷	3÷
315×		11+			2÷			
60×				448×			5−	4−
		3÷	1−					
1−				45×	2−		3−	5−
3÷		5−			3÷			

1008×		3−	18+	6×		11+		6+
4÷						11+		
		18+			16+			15+
12×		1−		1−		1−		
45×		10+		4÷		54×		12×
	48×		140×	4÷		5	9+	
13+				24+				17+
1−		15+			4−		1−	
			3÷		11+			

17+		49×		13+			4−	
	270×		17+	6×	8+		7+	56×
						19+		
21+		2−					144×	
		15×		5−		8		
1−	60×	6×		2÷	21+	17+		
			2÷				15+	
8	63×			18+	2÷	6−	16+	
12×								

40×	14+			22+		21+		
	576×				1−		3÷	
		7×		20+		16+		
28+			12+			112×		
				22+	6×		9	360×
63×		336×						
	1−	1−				448×		
			24+		3÷			5
9+					5−			

12×	10×	30+	16+		3−	270×		
			4−			6−		84×
8−			3−	2−				
12+				11+			22+	1−
	2−		2÷	4÷				
5−		14+			16+		13+	4−
280×			11+	13+				
		1−		21+		11+	3−	
	6						10×	

189×		13+		252×			3÷	
		21+						5−
60×	2÷		5−		35×		3−	
	2÷	1−		3−	10+			112×
		11+			6−			
1−	2−			15+	11+		15×	
	1−					1008×		
10+		13+	17+		14+			
						6	1−	

2÷	4−		21×		60×		24×	
	11+		8−			5−		18+
1−		6×	15+		24×			
	1−			192×			2−	
4−			16+			1−		12×
	7+			6−	24×			
		15+	48×		5−		1−	
3÷				5	56×			2÷
	15+		2÷		45×			

6−	96×		2−		8−		20+	
		14+	10+		5−	1−		
1−			1−				2÷	
4−		12×	5−		5−		2−	14+
2−	3−			8−		4−		
		5−	6+	48×	24×		1−	15+
3÷								
3÷		4	126×	90×		1−		
14+						12×		7

1

4²÷	2	6⁷⁺	1	3³	5⁹⁺
1²ˣ	3²⁻	5	2³÷	6	4
2	1	3⁷⁺	5²⁰ˣ	4	6³÷
6¹¹⁺	5	4	3³÷	1	2
3⁸⁺	4²÷	2	6¹¹⁺	5	1¹
5	6⁵⁻	1	4⁴	2¹⁻	3

2

3¹⁵ˣ	5	1⁵⁺	4	2³÷	6
4³²ˣ	2	6¹¹⁺	3¹⁵ˣ	5	1³⁺
1⁵⁻	4	5	6¹⁴⁺	3	2
6	3³÷	2²÷	5	1⁵⁻	4¹⁻
5⁵	1	4	2⁸ˣ	6	3
2¹¹⁺	6	3	1	4	5⁵

3

6⁵⁻	5⁴⁰ˣ	2	4²⁴ˣ	1³÷	3
1	3²÷	4	6	5²⁰ˣ	2³⁺
2⁴⁰ˣ	6	3¹⁵ˣ	5	4	1
5	4	1	3¹⁰⁺	2²	6²⁴ˣ
3⁶⁺	1	5	2	6¹⁴⁺	4
4⁴	2	6⁵⁻	1	3	5

4

6¹¹⁺	1²÷	4²÷	2	3³⁻	5¹⁻
5	2	3²÷	1⁴⁻	6	4
1³⁻	3¹⁴⁺	6	5	4²÷	2
4	5	2³÷	6	1²ˣ	3³
3⁶ˣ	6	5⁴⁻	4¹⁻	2	1
2	4⁴	1	3	5³⁰ˣ	6

118

Puzzle 5

3− 1	36× 6	3	2	60× 4	5
4	3− 2	5	5− 1	6	3
30× 2	1	10+ 4	15× 5	3	5− 6
5	1− 3	6	2÷ 4	2	1
3	4	2÷ 1	11+ 6	5	2 2
11+ 6	5	2	3 3	3− 1	4

Puzzle 6

3÷ 1	3	2 2	40× 4	11+ 6	5
13+ 4	6	5	2	4− 1	3÷ 3
3	12+ 2	4	6	5	1
3− 5	5− 1	6	15× 3	24× 2	4
2	120× 4	1	5	3	3÷ 6
6	5	3÷ 3	1	4 4	2

Puzzle 7

5− 1	12+ 5	3÷ 2	6	12× 3	4
6	3	4	3− 5	2	1
6× 2	1	3	2÷ 4	5− 6	90× 5
80× 5	4	6 6	2	1	3
4	180× 2	3× 1	3	1− 5	6
3	6	5	1	4	2 2

Puzzle 8

2÷ 4	2	1 1	120× 6	6× 3	4− 5
5− 6	15× 3	5	4	2	1
1	2− 4	2	5	5− 6	1− 3
8+ 5	432× 6	3	7+ 2	1	4
3	5 5	6	1	4	4− 2
3+ 2	1	4	2− 3	5	6

9

60× 4	5	3	3÷ 6	2	1 1
11+ 2	6	3÷ 1	3	20× 4	11+ 5
3	12× 4	2÷ 2	1	5	6
11+ 5	1	3÷ 6	2	1- 3	4
6	3	5 5	80× 4	5- 1	5+ 2
2÷ 1	2	4	5	6	3

10

1- 2	16+ 5	1	2- 6	4	3 3
3	6	4	5× 5	1	3- 2
24× 4	3	11+ 6	1	36× 2	5
5× 1	2	5	3 3	6	24× 4
5	1	5+ 2	2÷ 4	3	6
10+ 6	4	3	2	4- 5	1

11

6+ 3	1	2	4 4	1- 6	5
15+ 6	5	4	2× 2	1	2÷ 3
2÷ 2	15× 3	5	1	11+ 4	6
1	2÷ 4	5- 6	2÷ 3	5	2
20× 5	2	1	6	1- 3	5+ 4
4	6 6	2- 3	5	2	1

12

3- 3	6	60× 5	3+ 1	2	4 4
4× 1	2	4	10+ 3	11+ 6	11+ 5
2	30× 1	3	5	4	6
120× 4	5	6	2	1	9× 3
5	4 4	4- 2	6	3	1
6	3÷ 3	1	11+ 4	5	2

SOLUTIONS: 6×6 EASY

14

Puzzle 13

2 (3+)	1	4 (12+)	3	5	6 (6)
5 (4−)	3 (12+)	6 (3÷)	2	4 (16×)	1
1	2	3	5 (11+)	6	4
6 (72×)	4	5 (15×)	1	3	2 (1−)
4	5 (30×)	1 (2÷)	6 (2−)	2 (2)	3
3	6	2	4	1 (4−)	5

Puzzle 14

4 (4)	2 (3+)	1	6 (60×)	5	3 (72×)
5 (11+)	6	3 (36×)	1 (5×)	2	4
2 (2÷)	3	4	5	1	6
1	5 (14+)	6	3	4 (2÷)	2
6 (2−)	4	5 (9+)	2	3 (3÷)	1
3 (3÷)	1	2	4	6 (2−)	5 (5)

Puzzle 15

6 (2÷)	3	4 (4)	1 (10×)	5	2
1 (3÷)	5 (5)	2 (2−)	4	3 (2÷)	6
3	2 (10×)	5	6 (1−)	1 (3+)	4 (1−)
4 (2÷)	1 (5−)	6	5	2	3
2	4 (15+)	1 (3÷)	3 (2÷)	6	5 (6+)
5	6	3	2 (2÷)	4	1

Puzzle 16

3 (14+)	6	4 (16×)	2 (3−)	5	1 (10+)
5	2 (2)	1	4	3	6
2 (6×)	3	6 (5−)	1	4 (20×)	5
1 (6×)	4 (20×)	5	3 (2−)	6 (3÷)	2 (2÷)
6	1	3 (5+)	5	2	4
4 (1−)	5	2	6 (6)	1 (3÷)	3

17

11+ 5	6	2 2	6× 1	2− 4	15× 3
2÷ 4	3÷ 3	1	6	2	5
2	1	2÷ 6	3	5 5	2− 4
18× 3	20× 4	5	3+ 2	1	6
6	30× 2	13+ 4	5	3÷ 3	1
1	5	3	4	3÷ 6	2

18

2÷ 1	20× 4	11+ 6	5	1− 3	2
2	5	180× 3	6	1 1	1− 4
1− 4	2	5	5− 1	6	3
3	108× 6	3+ 1	40× 2	4	5
6	3	2	4	1− 5	4− 1
4− 5	1	4 4	3	3÷ 2	6

19

17+ 5	4	2× 1	6 6	24× 3	2
6	3 3	2	1	4	25× 5
2	13+ 6	3	4	5	1
2− 1	9+ 5	4	3÷ 2	6	7+ 3
3	3÷ 2	6	6+ 5	1	4
5+ 4	1	2− 5	3	4− 2	6

20

2÷ 2	4	4− 5	2÷ 3	6	3− 1
1− 3	3÷ 6	1	10+ 5	2	4
4	2	7+ 6	1	3	5 5
25× 1	5	3− 3	6	2÷ 4	2
5	24× 3	4	2	20× 1	2÷ 6
6 6	3+ 1	2	4	5	3

21

3 **3**	2÷ **4**	**2**	540× **6**	**5**	6+ **1**
30× **5**	**1**	**6**	5+ **4**	**3**	**2**
1- **2**	9+ **5**	**4**	**1**	**6**	**3**
1	2÷ **6**	**3**	3- **5**	2÷ **2**	**4**
12× **4**	**3**	9+ **5**	**2**	5- **1**	**6**
3÷ **6**	**2**	**1**	**3**	1- **4**	**5**

22

4- **6**	**2**	16× **1**	**4**	60× **5**	3÷ **3**
8+ **5**	**3**	**4**	**6**	**2**	**1**
2 **2**	120× **6**	90× **3**	3÷ **1**	40× **4**	**5**
1	**4**	**5**	**3**	6 **6**	**2**
1- **3**	**5**	**6**	6× **2**	**1**	2- **4**
4	10× **1**	**2**	**5**	**3**	**6**

23

4 **4**	13+ **2**	6× **1**	**6**	1- **5**	6× **3**
1- **3**	**5**	**6**	3× **1**	**4**	**2**
2	2÷ **6**	20× **5**	**3**	**1**	24× **4**
6+ **1**	**3**	**4**	3- **5**	**2**	**6**
5	24× **4**	**3**	3÷ **2**	**6**	**1**
5- **6**	**1**	**2**	60× **4**	**3**	**5**

24

10+ **5**	**1**	4 **4**	1- **2**	**3**	10+ **6**
3	48× **6**	**2**	25× **5**	**1**	**4**
1	**4**	2÷ **6**	**3**	**5**	8× **2**
2 **2**	2- **5**	**3**	2- **6**	**4**	**1**
72× **6**	**3**	10× **1**	**4**	30× **2**	**5**
4	**2**	**5**	5- **1**	**6**	**3**

25

16+ 4	5	2÷ 2	1	3− 3	6
1	6	3 3	120× 5	2− 2	4
11+ 2	3	4	6	9+ 5	1
6	5× 1	5	2÷ 2	4	3
8+ 3	12+ 2	1	4 4	11+ 6	5
5	4	6	6× 3	1	2

26

3− 1	14+ 3	40× 2	4	5	6 6
4	6	5	5− 1	2÷ 2	3÷ 3
2 2	2− 5	3	6	4	1
11+ 6	2÷ 4	5− 1	1− 2	2− 3	5
5	2	6	3	3− 1	4
12× 3	1	4	60× 5	6	2

27

3 3	3+ 1	1− 4	11+ 5	6	9+ 2
3÷ 6	2	5	3× 1	1− 4	3
2	720× 6	1	3	5	4
5+ 4	5	3 3	9+ 6	2	1
1	4	6	1− 2	3	1− 5
2− 5	3	7+ 2	4	1	6

28

2− 4	6	9+ 1	1− 2	3	90× 5
8+ 2	5	3	5− 1	2÷ 4	6
1	4 4	5	6	2	3
36× 6	3	2	4 4	6+ 5	1
2− 5	2÷ 1	13+ 4	3	3÷ 6	2
3	2	6	4− 5	1	4 4

29

1−2	5−1	5 5	2÷6	3	11+4
3	6	2÷4	2	5−1	5
5−1	40×4	15×3	5	6	2
6	5	2	1−3	2−4	5−1
9+5	1−3	7+1	4	2	6
4	2	6	9+1	5	3

30

2÷4	2	5−6	1	30×5	3
1−3	6×1	15+5	4	6	2
2	6	1	2÷3	1−4	5
20×5	3 3	2÷4	6	6×2	1
1	4	2	10×5	3	2−6
90×6	5	3	2	1 1	4

31

3÷2	6	20×1	12+4	5	3
12×3	4	5	5−1	6	2÷2
4	30×5	6	1−2	3	1
4−1	8+3	3÷2	6	2÷4	1−5
5	1	4	8+3	2	6
6 6	1−2	3	5	5+1	4

32

12+4	5	3	30×6	12×1	2 2
4−2	6	1	5	3	4
5−1	10+3	2÷4	2	1−6	5
6	2	5	16×1	4	3−3
2−3	2÷1	2	4	5 5	6
5	2−4	6	6×3	2	1

33

3− 6	4− 1	24× 4	2	3	12+ 5
3	5	2 2	180× 6	12+ 1	4
4− 1	4 4	6	5	2	3
5	1− 2	3	3÷ 1	4	3÷ 6
11+ 4	6	1	3	5	2
1− 2	3	1− 5	4	5− 6	1

34

11+ 6	5	3+ 1	2	1− 4	3
2÷ 4	2	2÷ 3	6	4− 5	1
1− 2	24× 6	4	3÷ 3	1	1− 5
3	1	60× 5	1− 4	1− 2	6
15× 1	4 4	6	5	3	2÷ 2
5	3	2	5− 1	6	4

35

11+ 5	24× 4	1	6	2÷ 2	60× 3
6	9+ 3	3− 2	5	1	4
3÷ 1	2	4	2÷ 3	6	5
3	1− 6	5	1− 1	1− 4	2 2
9+ 4	5	3− 6	2	3	7+ 1
2÷ 2	1	3	9+ 4	5	6

36

12× 4	3	7+ 2	5	3+ 1	2− 6
5− 6	1− 5	3÷ 1	3	2	4
1	6	10+ 4	2	1− 5	3÷ 3
7+ 5	2÷ 2	18× 3	4	6	1
2	4	6	1	14+ 3	5
3÷ 3	1	11+ 5	6	4	2

126

37

2 (3÷)	4 (4)	3 (9+)	5 (4−)	1	6 (13+)
6	5	1	3 (10+)	2	4
1 (5−)	6	4 (2÷)	2	5	3
5 (11+)	3 (5+)	2	6 (36×)	4 (5+)	1
4	2	6	1	3 (10+)	5
3 (2−)	1	5 (120×)	4	6	2

38

6 (9+)	3 (2−)	5	4 (2−)	2	1 (15×)
2	1	4 (120×)	5	6	3
3 (1−)	6 (5−)	1	2 (5+)	4 (4)	5
4	5 (5)	2	1	3 (2−)	6 (2−)
1 (6+)	2 (2÷)	6 (12+)	3	5	4
5	4	3	6 (6)	1 (1−)	2

39

3 (11+)	6 (2−)	4	2 (2÷)	1	5 (1−)
1	5	2 (15+)	4	3	6
2	4 (1−)	3	6	5 (4−)	1
6 (15+)	1 (3×)	5 (13+)	3	2 (3÷)	4 (2÷)
4	3	1	5	6	2
5	2 (12×)	6	1	4 (1−)	3

40

1 (3÷)	3	6 (1−)	4 (1−)	5	2 (10+)
2 (2÷)	4	5	1 (2÷)	6 (7+)	3
4 (1−)	6 (5−)	3 (6×)	2	1	5
5	1	2	6 (72×)	3	4
3 (11+)	2	1 (6+)	5	4 (11+)	6
6	5 (1−)	4	3 (1−)	2	1

127

41

6× 2	1	5 5	2− 6	4	2− 3
3	2− 6	1− 4	2÷ 2	1	5
1− 5	4	3	5− 1	6	2÷ 2
6	2÷ 2	1	2− 3	5	4
4− 1	5	2÷ 2	4	10+ 3	6
7+ 4	3	1− 6	5	2 2	1

42

9+ 2	3	120× 5	4	6	1 1
4	48× 6	1	10+ 2	3	5
12+ 5	4	2	18× 6	1	3
6	1	15+ 3	5	2÷ 2	4
2− 3	5	6	1	1− 4	3÷ 2
2÷ 1	2	12× 4	3	5	6

43

30× 3	5	11+ 6	10+ 1	1− 4	2 2
2	4	1	5	3	9+ 6
6+ 5	3÷ 6	3 3	4	2	1
1	2	1− 4	3	1− 6	5
10+ 6	6× 3	13+ 5	2	4− 1	1− 4
4	1	2	6	5	3

44

12+ 1	6	10+ 2	3	5	4 4
60× 3	5	2÷ 4	2	6× 1	6
5	4	6× 3	11+ 6	2 2	1
12+ 6	2	1	4	16+ 3	5
4	2− 3	16+ 5	1	6	2
2	1	6	5	1− 4	3

45

30× 6	1 1	1− 3	4	8+ 5	2
5	15+ 2	4	2÷ 6	3	1
5+ 4	3	6	1− 2	5− 1	1− 5
1	12+ 5	2÷ 2	3	6	4
3	4	1	6+ 5	2÷ 2	3− 6
13+ 2	6	5	1	4	3

46

4− 1	5	48× 4	2	90× 6	3
5+ 3	2	6	12× 4	5	1
14+ 6	1	2	3	13+ 4	5
12× 4	3	5	1− 6	1	96× 2
7+ 2	3− 4	1	5	3	6
5	6 6	3÷ 3	1	2	4

47

15+ 5	6	4	30× 2	3	1
1− 2	3	15+ 1	5	5+ 4	2÷ 6
24× 4	8+ 2	5	6	1	3
6	1	3	1− 4	3− 2	5
1	5	12× 2	3	1− 6	2÷ 4
7+ 3	4	6	1	5	2

48

2÷ 2	4	5 5	36× 3	12+ 6	1
3÷ 1	3	6	2	5	16+ 4
180× 6	2	4× 4	1	3	5
3	5	1	12+ 6	4	1− 2
1− 4	5− 6	1− 2	5	1	3
5	1	3	12+ 4	2	6

129

49

2	3	4	6	1	5
6	1	5	3	4	2
5	4	6	1	2	3
3	2	1	5	6	4
1	5	2	4	3	6
4	6	3	2	5	1

50

4	5	6	2	3	1
1	2	3	4	6	5
6	1	2	3	5	4
5	3	4	1	2	6
2	6	1	5	4	3
3	4	5	6	1	2

51

2	5	9	7	8	6	1	3	4
1	3	7	9	2	4	8	6	5
8	4	6	5	3	1	2	7	9
4	9	3	8	1	2	6	5	7
5	2	8	4	6	7	9	1	3
6	7	1	3	5	9	4	8	2
7	8	4	1	9	5	3	2	6
3	6	5	2	4	8	7	9	1
9	1	2	6	7	3	5	4	8

52

2	4	6	9	5	1	3	7	8
7	5	8	6	2	3	9	4	1
9	1	3	8	7	4	2	5	6
3	6	5	7	8	9	1	2	4
8	7	4	2	1	5	6	9	3
1	2	9	4	3	6	5	8	7
5	8	7	3	6	2	4	1	9
4	3	2	1	9	7	8	6	5
6	9	1	5	4	8	7	3	2

53

18+ 9	3	4÷ 8	2	1512× 7	6	7× 1	60× 5	4
2÷ 2	6	25× 5	9	4	1	7	3	6- 8
4	1- 7	1	5	36× 3	2- 8	6	63× 9	2
15× 5	8	6- 9	3	6	2	18+ 4	7	8- 1
3	4 4	14× 2	7	1	60× 5	8	6	9
8+ 7	3+ 1	192× 6	8	9	4	3	2 2	90× 5
1	2	4	5- 6	12× 5	7	17+ 9	8	3
1- 8	9	10+ 7	1	4÷ 2	8+ 3	5	28× 4	6
30× 6	5	3	4 4	8	7- 9	2	1	7

54

84× 7	3	432× 8	14+ 5	9	2÷ 2	4	5- 6	1
3+ 2	4	9	21× 7	5- 6	1	240× 5	8	3
1	11+ 5	6	3	2÷ 4	5- 8	2	81× 9	140× 7
4	6	5- 7	3÷ 2	8	3	9	1	5
15× 5	17+ 9	2	6	4- 1	7	15+ 8	12+ 3	4
3	8	9× 1	9	5	2- 4	6	7	2
23+ 9	3- 2	5	1	1- 3	6 6	11+ 7	4	240× 8
8	7	8+ 3	12× 4	4- 2	9	1	5	6
6	1	4	8	7	2- 5	3 3	7- 2	9

55

17+ 8	90× 5	3	8- 9	56× 7	4	6× 1	6	5+ 2
9	7 7	6	1	240× 8	2	1- 5	4	3
3+ 1	2	3- 4	5	6	135× 3	15+ 7	8	17+ 9
3- 2	5- 1	7	2÷ 4	5	9	2÷ 6	8- 3	8
5	6	24+ 9	2	17+ 3	8	2÷ 4	1	7 7
12× 4	3	8	7	4× 1	6	2	9	60× 5
42× 7	4- 8	30× 5	3	4	1	3÷ 9	2	6
6	4	2	72× 8	9	12+ 5	3	12+ 7	1
3 3	8- 9	1	3÷ 6	2	7	3- 8	5	4

56

40× 5	8	270× 9	2÷ 1	2	16+ 7	6	3	4÷ 4
3+ 3	28× 4	6	5	72× 8	9	9+ 2	7	1
1	7	2÷ 2	1- 3	4	14+ 6	5	7- 9	17+ 8
10+ 4	6	1	35× 7	5	3	56× 8	2	9
5- 2	17+ 5	72× 8	9	2- 6	4	7	6+ 1	2÷ 3
7	9	3	15+ 8	1	2 2	16× 4	5	6
432× 9	3+ 2	7 7	6	11+ 3	8	1	4	2- 5
8	1	12+ 4	2÷ 2	16+ 9	2- 5	3	6 6	7
6	3	5	4	7	8- 1	9	6- 8	2

57

3+ 2	3÷ 9	3	28× 4	7	3÷ 6	8− 1	13+ 8	5
1	56× 8	7	2− 5	3	2	9	3÷ 6	12× 4
1− 5	4	17+ 6	8	8− 9	1	140× 7	2	3
17+ 9	3+ 1	2	3	2− 6	8	4	5	13+ 7
8	2÷ 3	11+ 4	7	2÷ 1	90× 5	2	9	6
84× 7	6	16+ 5	9	2	12+ 4	14+ 8	3× 3	1
4	5− 7	9 9	2	5	3	6	1	1− 8
3	2	6× 1	6	20+ 8	7	5	4 4	9
240× 6	5	8	1	5− 4	9	10+ 3	7	2 2

58

28× 7	2− 8	3÷ 2	6	3+ 1	15× 3	1− 4	17+ 9	35× 5
4	6	9 9	28× 7	2	5	3	8	1
9× 1	3	13+ 5	4	17+ 9	8	3÷ 6	2	7
3	7	1	3÷ 2	6	9	13+ 8	1− 5	6+ 4
80× 2	17+ 9	8	2− 3	5	4	7	1	2− 6
5	4	14+ 6	8	1− 7	1	8− 9	3	5+ 2
8	5 5	4	8− 1	3	5− 6	60× 2	126× 7	9
15+ 6	2÷ 1	105× 7	9	8	2	5	15+ 4	3
9	2	3	5	28× 4	7	1	6 6	8

59

2− 4	5− 2	8+ 5	3	8− 9	1	21+ 8	6	7
6	7	4÷ 8	2	4 4	8+ 5	3	8− 9	1
9× 1	9	2÷ 3	6	1− 7	8	3− 2	5	2− 4
216× 3	1	2 2	40× 5	8	126× 9	1− 4	1− 7	6
9	140× 4	6× 6	1	2	7	5	8	3 3
8	5	7	7+ 4	3	2÷ 6	2× 1	2	11+ 9
5 5	4− 8	4	3− 9	6	3	42× 7	1	2
5− 7	2÷ 3	8− 9	56× 8	6+ 1	2÷ 2	6	160× 4	5
2	6	1	7	5	4	3÷ 9	3	8

60

11+ 5	6	42× 7	2	3	2÷ 8	4	17+ 9	10+ 1
3+ 2	1− 4	15+ 9	6	8− 1	175× 5	7 7	8	3
1	3	8	2÷ 4	9	7	5	14× 2	6
10+ 4	4÷ 8	2	1− 7	90× 5	3	6	1	45× 9
6	12+ 9	3	8	10+ 4	4× 1	2	7	5
15+ 7	5	8− 1	9	6	2	7+ 3	4	336× 8
3	2÷ 1	20× 4	5	11+ 2	9	17+ 8	6	7
8 8	2	4− 5	1	1− 7	11+ 6	9	60× 3	4
2− 9	7	2÷ 6	3	8	4	1	5	2 2

61

6	3	4	2	1	8	9	7	5
1	9	8	6	7	5	3	2	4
5	7	2	9	3	4	8	1	6
2	5	3	8	6	9	1	4	7
8	6	7	5	4	1	2	9	3
9	4	1	3	2	7	6	5	8
4	8	6	7	9	2	5	3	1
3	1	9	4	5	6	7	8	2
7	2	5	1	8	3	4	6	9

62

2	5	8	7	1	9	3	6	4
7	6	9	8	3	4	1	2	5
3	1	4	5	6	2	8	9	7
9	8	7	4	2	6	5	1	3
6	2	1	3	8	5	7	4	9
5	4	3	9	7	1	6	8	2
4	7	5	6	9	8	2	3	1
1	9	6	2	5	3	4	7	8
8	3	2	1	4	7	9	5	6

63

4	7	3	1	2	5	6	8	9
1	2	8	6	7	9	5	3	4
9	6	5	3	4	8	2	7	1
6	9	4	5	1	3	8	2	7
8	3	2	7	6	4	1	9	5
7	5	1	9	8	2	3	4	6
2	1	7	8	9	6	4	5	3
5	4	6	2	3	7	9	1	8
3	8	9	4	5	1	7	6	2

64

8	7	2	1	4	9	6	5	3
9	6	4	7	5	3	2	1	8
3	5	1	8	2	6	4	9	7
7	4	6	2	8	5	1	3	9
1	3	8	9	7	4	5	6	2
5	2	9	3	6	1	8	7	4
4	9	5	6	3	8	7	2	1
2	8	3	5	1	7	9	4	6
6	1	7	4	9	2	3	8	5

65

5-	72×		3÷		17+	3÷	6+	13+
7	6	4	3	1	8	2	5	9
2	3	20+ 8	5	7	9	6	1	4
8- 9	25× 5	1	4- 6	2	96× 4	17+ 8	10+ 7	3
1	2 2	5	84× 7	8	3	9	120× 4	6
17+ 8	9	6	2	1- 4	6- 1	7	5- 3	5
3 3	14+ 4	7	8- 9	5	6	1	8	15+ 2
160× 4	8	3	1	11+ 9	2	5 5	6	7
5	8- 1	9	2÷ 4	2÷ 6	35× 7	48× 3	2	8
84× 6	7	2	8	3	5	36× 4	9	1

66

3+	2÷		3-		64×	315×		36×
1	3	6	4	7	8	9	5	2
2	140× 4	72× 9	2- 5	3	1	8	7	6
7	5	8	15+ 6	9	2÷ 2	4	1 1	3
17+ 9	3÷ 6	1	2 2	12+ 4	3	5	144× 8	6- 7
8	2	14+ 4	21+ 7	5	9	6	3	1
2- 5	7	3	64× 8	1	6 6	5- 2	36× 9	4
3	3+ 1	2	9	8	140× 4	7	60× 6	5
2- 4	13+ 8	5	1	36× 6	7	3÷ 3	2	288× 9
6	63× 9	7	3	2	5	1	4	8

67

1-	17+	1-		18×	3-		4÷	
3	9	6	5	1	7	4	8	2
2	8	140× 7	6	3	20× 4	5	10+ 9	1
5× 1	4	5	7+ 2	9 9	17+ 8	2÷ 6	3	17+ 7
5	1	2	3	1- 7	9	6- 8	6	4
6 6	189× 7	9	16× 4	8	90× 5	2	15× 1	3
17+ 8	3	4	1	12+ 6	2	9	15+ 7	5
9	15+ 5	64× 8	7 7	4	9× 1	3	2	6
4	6	1	8	2	3	16+ 7	5	17+ 9
9+ 7	2	3÷ 3	9	11+ 5	6	1 1	4	8

68

20×			14+	3-	3÷		7	5-
4	5	1	6	2	3	9	7	8
378× 9	7	6	8	5	16× 4	1	60× 2	3
42× 2	17+ 8	9× 3	1	2- 7	9	4	6	5
7	9	11+ 4	3	2- 6	64× 1	8	3- 5	2
3	6 6	5	2	4	8	10+ 7	20+ 1	9
192× 8	3+ 1	2	7 7	9	5	3	4	6
6	4	15+ 7	5- 9	30× 3	2	5	17+ 8	6- 1
15× 5	3	8	4	5- 1	6	2 2	9	7
3+ 1	2	22+ 9	5	8	7	1- 6	3	1- 4

134

69

¹⁵⁺7	¹⁸⁰ˣ5	9	¹⁷⁺8	²2	⁹ˣ3	¹³⁺4	1	¹¹⁺6
2	6	4	9	¹⁻7	1	3	8	5
³ˣ1	3	⁵⁻8	¹¹⁺4	6	⁵⁻5	¹⁴⁺7	2	⁷⁻9
²⁰⁺9	1	3	7	5	4	¹⁴⁺8	6	2
4	7	⁴⁻6	2	¹⁷⁺8	9	¹⁴⁺5	²¹ˣ3	1
¹⁹⁺5	⁸8	³⁺2	1	²÷3	6	9	¹⁻4	7
6	²÷2	¹⁸⁹ˣ7	3	9	⁵⁶ˣ8	1	5	¹⁻4
8	4	²⁵ˣ5	²⁴ˣ6	1	7	¹⁰⁸ˣ2	9	3
⁶⁻3	9	1	5	4	²2	6	¹⁵⁺7	8

70

²÷6	3	¹⁴⁺5	9	¹¹⁺7	4	³⁺1	2	²⁴⁺8
⁸8	¹⁰⁸ˣ4	9	3	³⁺1	2	¹¹⁺6	5	7
⁵⁻7	¹¹⁺2	³⁶ˣ1	6	²⁰⁰ˣ5	8	²⁸ˣ4	⁹ˣ3	9
2	9	6	¹⁷⁺4	⁸8	5	7	1	3
³⁺3	¹²⁺5	²÷4	7	6	⁸¹ˣ1	9	⁶⁻8	2
1	7	8	¹⁻2	3	9	¹⁻5	4	²⁴ˣ6
²³⁺9	6	²2	¹²⁺5	4	3	¹⁻8	7	1
¹⁻5	8	²¹ˣ3	⁹⁺1	⁶³ˣ9	7	³÷2	6	4
4	1	7	8	¹¹⁺2	6	3	⁴⁻9	5

71

⁹⁰ˣ5	3	6	⁵⁻9	4	1	⁸ˣ2	⁹⁺7	⁹⁶⁰ˣ8
²⁵²ˣ7	9	³⁺2	⁸⁺5	3	8	1	4	6
4	⁸8	1	⁵⁻7	²÷2	6	²÷3	²⁷⁺9	5
¹⁵ˣ3	¹⁰⁺6	4	2	1	⁴⁻9	5	8	7
1	5	¹⁷⁺9	²÷6	³⁻8	¹³⁺7	4	2	3
⁹⁺2	7	8	3	5	¹⁶⁸ˣ4	6	⁸⁻1	9
¹⁷⁺8	²÷4	⁶⁺5	1	³÷9	3	7	⁹⁺6	2
9	2	³⁻7	4	¹⁻6	¹³⁺5	8	⁵⁴⁰ˣ3	1
⁵⁻6	1	²⁴ˣ3	8	7	²2	9	5	4

72

¹³⁺7	¹⁸⁺9	5	²⁶⁺8	³⁺2	1	¹³⁺4	3	6
2	3	4	6	¹⁴⁰ˣ7	5	¹⁷⁺8	9	⁶⁻1
1	¹⁴⁺6	8	3	9	4	⁵5	¹⁰ˣ2	7
²⁰ˣ4	¹⁶⁺7	9	⁴⁸ˣ2	3	8	³⁻6	1	5
5	²÷2	²¹ˣ3	7	1	⁶6	9	²¹⁺8	4
¹⁷⁺8	1	¹⁻6	¹⁻5	4	9	³÷3	7	2
9	¹⁶⁰ˣ4	7	⁴⁻1	5	⁶ˣ3	2	²⁻6	8
²÷3	8	¹²⁺2	4	6	⁴⁹ˣ7	1	²⁰ˣ5	³÷9
6	5	⁸⁻1	9	⁴÷8	2	7	4	3

73

2	5	1	8	4	3	6	7	9
7	9	4	2	1	6	3	5	8
6	8	3	9	5	7	1	4	2
4	1	6	5	2	8	9	3	7
3	2	5	4	7	9	8	1	6
9	7	8	6	3	1	4	2	5
1	6	7	3	9	5	2	8	4
5	4	9	1	8	2	7	6	3
8	3	2	7	6	4	5	9	1

74

1	8	3	7	5	4	2	9	6
5	7	2	9	6	1	3	4	8
6	9	4	3	2	8	5	7	1
4	5	1	2	9	3	6	8	7
3	2	7	4	8	6	9	1	5
8	6	9	5	1	7	4	3	2
7	4	5	1	3	2	8	6	9
2	1	8	6	4	9	7	5	3
9	3	6	8	7	5	1	2	4

75

5	6	8	9	3	1	2	4	7
4	2	3	6	5	7	1	9	8
9	1	7	8	4	2	3	5	6
6	5	1	2	8	9	7	3	4
8	3	2	5	7	4	6	1	9
7	4	9	1	6	3	5	8	2
2	9	5	7	1	8	4	6	3
1	8	4	3	2	6	9	7	5
3	7	6	4	9	5	8	2	1

76

8	6	9	5	1	3	2	7	4
3	4	1	2	8	7	6	9	5
5	2	7	6	9	4	8	3	1
9	1	8	3	5	2	7	4	6
4	5	3	1	7	6	9	8	2
6	7	2	8	4	9	5	1	3
1	3	6	7	2	8	4	5	9
7	9	5	4	6	1	3	2	8
2	8	4	9	3	5	1	6	7

77

6	1	5	8	2	4	9	7	3
8	3	2	5	7	9	1	4	6
4	9	7	3	1	6	8	5	2
2	7	8	1	3	5	6	9	4
9	5	4	6	8	2	3	1	7
1	6	3	9	4	7	2	8	5
5	4	9	2	6	1	7	3	8
3	2	1	7	5	8	4	6	9
7	8	6	4	9	3	5	2	1

78

9	7	8	3	6	2	5	4	1
5	6	1	4	9	8	7	2	3
2	4	3	1	5	7	6	9	8
7	9	4	5	8	3	1	6	2
6	8	2	9	4	1	3	5	7
3	1	5	7	2	6	4	8	9
1	5	9	2	3	4	8	7	6
4	3	6	8	7	9	2	1	5
8	2	7	6	1	5	9	3	4

79

3	5	8	1	2	6	4	9	7
4	2	1	5	9	7	8	6	3
6	7	9	4	8	3	1	5	2
1	3	4	7	6	9	2	8	5
8	6	7	2	5	1	9	3	4
2	9	5	8	3	4	6	7	1
9	8	2	3	1	5	7	4	6
7	1	3	6	4	8	5	2	9
5	4	6	9	7	2	3	1	8

80

7	2	3	4	8	5	9	6	1
1	6	4	2	7	9	5	3	8
9	8	5	6	1	3	7	4	2
2	5	8	3	4	7	6	1	9
3	1	7	9	5	6	8	2	4
6	4	9	8	2	1	3	5	7
5	7	6	1	9	4	2	8	3
4	3	2	7	6	8	1	9	5
8	9	1	5	3	2	4	7	6

81

3	2	9	8	1	5	6	7	4
5	7	1	9	4	6	8	2	3
8	6	4	2	3	7	5	9	1
6	9	7	4	2	3	1	8	5
4	8	2	1	5	9	3	6	7
1	5	3	6	7	8	2	4	9
2	4	6	5	9	1	7	3	8
9	3	5	7	8	2	4	1	6
7	1	8	3	6	4	9	5	2

82

4	8	7	6	5	2	1	9	3
3	2	1	4	7	9	5	6	8
6	9	5	3	1	8	4	7	2
5	1	9	2	8	6	7	3	4
8	7	4	5	9	3	2	1	6
2	6	3	1	4	7	9	8	5
9	3	2	7	6	4	8	5	1
7	5	6	8	2	1	3	4	9
1	4	8	9	3	5	6	2	7

83

7	3	2	4	8	1	5	6	9
6	5	4	3	2	9	1	7	8
8	9	1	7	5	6	2	4	3
3	7	5	9	6	4	8	1	2
2	8	6	1	3	5	4	9	7
4	1	9	2	7	8	3	5	6
9	4	8	6	1	2	7	3	5
5	6	3	8	4	7	9	2	1
1	2	7	5	9	3	6	8	4

84

9	4	2	5	7	3	6	8	1
1	3	5	6	8	9	4	2	7
8	7	6	4	1	2	9	5	3
2	5	7	3	4	8	1	6	9
6	9	4	1	2	7	5	3	8
3	1	8	9	6	5	2	7	4
4	2	9	8	3	6	7	1	5
7	8	1	2	5	4	3	9	6
5	6	3	7	9	1	8	4	2

SOLUTIONS: 9×9 MEDIUM

85

4	7	6	3	5	2	9	8	1
8	5	1	4	9	7	6	2	3
2	9	3	1	6	8	4	7	5
7	8	4	5	2	1	3	6	9
5	3	2	6	7	9	1	4	8
6	1	9	8	3	4	7	5	2
9	2	5	7	1	6	8	3	4
1	6	8	2	4	3	5	9	7
3	4	7	9	8	5	2	1	6

86

2	3	1	7	6	5	9	8	4
4	9	5	1	3	8	6	2	7
8	7	6	9	2	4	5	3	1
1	5	7	4	9	2	8	6	3
9	6	4	8	5	3	7	1	2
3	8	2	6	1	7	4	9	5
5	1	9	2	7	6	3	4	8
6	4	3	5	8	1	2	7	9
7	2	8	3	4	9	1	5	6

87

4	5	6	3	1	7	8	9	2
1	3	2	5	8	9	6	4	7
9	8	7	6	2	4	5	3	1
2	1	4	9	7	6	3	8	5
8	6	5	4	3	2	1	7	9
7	9	3	8	5	1	4	2	6
5	2	1	7	4	8	9	6	3
6	7	8	1	9	3	2	5	4
3	4	9	2	6	5	7	1	8

88

1	4	7	6	8	2	9	3	5
9	5	3	1	7	4	6	2	8
6	2	8	9	5	3	1	4	7
7	1	5	2	3	6	8	9	4
3	8	6	5	4	9	7	1	2
4	9	2	8	1	7	5	6	3
5	3	4	7	6	1	2	8	9
8	6	9	3	2	5	4	7	1
2	7	1	4	9	8	3	5	6

SOLUTIONS: 9×9 MEDIUM

89

3÷ 3	9	12+ 7	5	3− 4	1	1− 6	4÷ 2	8
3+ 2	17+ 8	4	17+ 6	10+ 7	3	5	17+ 9	1
1	5	36× 6	2	9	8	4	1− 3	7
4− 5	6	1	1− 3	2	7	8	4	15+ 9
9	2÷ 2	5− 3	8	1− 5	4	2− 1	7 7	6
42× 7	4	1− 8	9	1 1	6	3− 3	10× 5	2
6	4− 1	5	14+ 7	3	2	17+ 9	8	1− 4
2÷ 8	42× 3	2	4	54× 6	9	6− 7	1	5
4	7	8− 9	1	3− 8	5	3÷ 2	6	3 3

90

560× 5	2	336× 4	7	3÷ 3	1	29+ 6	8	9
7	8	3	4	25+ 9	6	5	1	5− 2
3− 9	6	1	2	5	14+ 8	1− 3	4	7
2− 6	4	504× 7	3	3+ 2	5	1	9 9	2− 8
30× 3	5	9	8	1	16+ 7	2÷ 4	2	6
2	3× 1	4032× 8	6	33+ 4	9	15+ 7	5	3
1	3	2	9	7	4− 4	8	1− 6	5
4 4	7	6	5	8	2	7− 9	42× 3	3− 1
17+ 8	9	6+ 5	1	2+ 6	3	2	7	4

SOLUTIONS: 9×9 DIFFICULT

91

1− 2	3	49× 1	7	2− 4	14+ 8	5	15+ 9	2÷ 6
1− 8	9	7	4− 5	6	1	2	4	3
1− 6	11+ 4	5	9	1− 3	2	14+ 1	7	1− 8
5	2	9+ 8	1	3− 7	4	6	11+ 3	9
3− 7	5− 1	24× 3	8	162× 9	6	2÷ 4	2	5
4	6	72× 9	2	25× 5	3	8	1	84× 7
8− 9	8	4	11+ 3	1	5	26+ 7	6	2
1	7	2	6	8	9	3	18+ 5	4
2− 3	5	6 6	2÷ 4	2	7	9	8	1

92

48× 8	3	7	18+ 9	5	10+ 4	6	2÷ 1	2
2	6	5	8	3	1	1− 4	1− 9	45× 7
108× 4	10+ 1	9	1− 7	6	2	3	5	15+ 8
3	9	17+ 6	5	2	56× 8	1	7	1− 4
5 5	14× 2	14+ 8	4	6− 1	7	3− 9	6	3
56× 1	7	4	54× 6	9	16+ 3	8	3− 2	5
7	8	2	1	2− 4	6	5	3 3	23+ 9
3− 9	3− 4	1	13+ 3	35× 7	5	18+ 2	8	6
6	2− 5	3	2	8	9	7	4÷ 4	1

93

2	6	7	9	4	5	1	3	8
9	4	5	8	1	3	2	7	6
1	3	8	6	2	7	5	9	4
8	1	2	5	6	9	7	4	3
5	9	6	7	3	4	8	2	1
3	7	4	1	8	2	9	6	5
4	5	3	2	7	8	6	1	9
7	8	1	3	9	6	4	5	2
6	2	9	4	5	1	3	8	7

94

8	9	3	2	6	1	4	7	5
4	7	6	8	3	5	2	9	1
1	2	5	4	9	7	6	3	8
3	4	8	9	5	6	1	2	7
5	1	7	3	8	2	9	6	4
9	6	2	7	1	4	5	8	3
2	3	4	5	7	9	8	1	6
6	8	9	1	4	3	7	5	2
7	5	1	6	2	8	3	4	9

95

2	8	1	7	6	4	3	5	9
4	6	7	9	3	5	2	1	8
3	9	5	8	2	1	4	6	7
7	4	8	6	1	9	5	2	3
9	1	3	5	7	2	8	4	6
6	5	2	3	4	8	9	7	1
5	3	4	1	8	7	6	9	2
8	7	9	2	5	6	1	3	4
1	2	6	4	9	3	7	8	5

96

4	3	9	2	6	7	5	8	1
5	1	8	3	9	4	7	6	2
2	6	7	1	8	5	4	3	9
6	4	1	5	3	9	8	2	7
8	5	3	4	7	2	1	9	6
7	9	2	6	1	8	3	5	4
9	8	5	7	4	6	2	1	3
1	7	6	8	2	3	9	4	5
3	2	4	9	5	1	6	7	8

97

¹²ˣ3	¹⁰ˣ2	³⁰⁺8	¹⁶⁺9	7	³⁻4	²⁷⁰ˣ5	1	6
4	5	7	⁴⁻2	6	1	8	9	⁸⁴ˣ⁶⁻3
⁸⁻9	1	6	³⁻8	²⁻5	3	2	7	4
¹²⁺6	4	9	5	¹¹⁺8	2	1	²²⁺3	¹⁻7
2	²⁻7	5	²÷3	⁴÷1	9	6	4	8
⁵⁻8	3	¹⁴⁺1	6	4	¹⁶⁺7	9	¹³⁺2	⁴⁻5
²⁸⁰ˣ5	9	4	¹¹⁺7	¹³⁺2	6	3	8	1
1	8	¹⁻2	4	²¹⁺3	5	¹¹⁺7	³⁻6	9
7	⁶6	3	1	9	8	4	¹⁰ˣ5	2

98

¹⁸⁹ˣ3	1	¹³⁺5	8	²⁵²ˣ9	4	7	³÷2	6
7	9	²¹⁺6	5	2	3	1	4	⁵⁻8
⁶⁰ˣ2	²÷8	4	⁵⁻6	1	³⁵ˣ7	5	³⁻9	3
5	²÷2	¹⁻3	4	³⁻8	¹⁰⁺1	9	6	¹¹²ˣ7
6	4	¹¹⁺1	7	5	⁶⁻9	3	8	2
¹⁻8	²⁻7	9	3	¹⁵⁺6	¹¹⁺2	4	¹⁵ˣ1	5
9	¹⁻6	7	2	4	5	¹⁰⁰⁸ˣ8	3	1
¹⁰⁺4	5	¹³⁺8	¹⁷⁺1	3	¹⁴⁺6	2	7	9
1	3	2	9	7	8	⁶6	¹⁻5	4

99

²÷4	⁴⁻5	9	²¹ˣ3	7	⁶⁰ˣ2	6	²⁴ˣ1	8
8	¹¹⁺2	6	⁸⁻9	1	5	⁵⁻7	3	¹⁸⁺4
¹⁻7	3	⁶ˣ1	¹⁵⁺4	6	²⁴ˣ8	2	9	5
6	¹⁻8	2	5	¹⁹²ˣ4	1	3	²⁻7	9
⁴⁻1	9	3	¹⁶⁺7	8	6	¹⁻4	5	¹²ˣ2
5	⁷⁺4	7	2	⁶⁻9	²⁴ˣ3	8	6	1
2	1	¹⁵⁺5	⁴⁸ˣ6	3	⁵⁻4	9	¹⁻8	7
³⁺9	6	4	8	⁵5	⁵⁶ˣ7	1	2	²÷3
3	¹⁵⁺7	8	²÷1	2	⁴⁵ˣ9	5	4	6

100

⁶⁻7	⁹⁶ˣ2	6	²⁻3	5	1	⁸⁻9	8	²⁰⁺4
1	8	¹⁴⁺9	¹⁰⁺6	4	⁵⁻2	¹⁻7	5	3
¹⁻4	3	5	¹⁻8	9	7	6	²÷1	2
⁴⁻9	5	¹²ˣ1	⁵⁻2	7	8	3	²⁻4	¹⁴⁺6
²⁻6	³⁻7	3	⁸⁻4	1	9	⁴⁻5	2	8
8	4	⁵⁻2	⁶⁺5	6	⁴⁸ˣ3	²⁴ˣ1	7	¹⁵⁺9
³÷3	9	7	1	8	4	2	6	5
³÷2	6	⁴4	¹²⁶ˣ7	3	⁹⁰ˣ5	8	¹⁻9	1
¹⁴⁺5	1	8	9	2	6	¹²ˣ4	3	⁷7

Bonus 9×9 KenKen Puzzle without symbols

The rules for playing KenKen™ are fairly simple:

1. For a 9X9 puzzle, fill in with the numbers 1-9.
2. Do not repeat a number in any row or column.
3. The numbers in each heavily outlined set of squares, called cages, must combine (in any order) to produce the target number in the top corner of the cage using any of the mathematical operations (addition, subtraction, multiplication and division). You must work out which operation is used in each cage!

Cages with just one box should be filled in with the target number in the top corner. A digit can be repeated within a cage as long as it is not in the same row or column.

1701			16	4	105	7	1152	
175								
		31			48			
30	14			448		11		
		525					4536	
			4860	8				
3072			6	1944		3675		

KENKEN SOLUTION

¹⁷⁰¹3	7	9	¹⁶2	⁴1	¹⁰⁵5	⁷8	¹¹⁵²6	4
¹⁷⁵5	9	2	4	3	7	1	8	6
1	5	7	³¹9	8	3	⁴⁸6	4	2
³⁰9	¹⁴4	6	8	⁴⁴⁸7	2	¹¹5	3	1
6	1	⁵²⁵3	5	4	8	2	⁴⁵³⁶9	7
8	3	5	7	⁴⁸⁶⁰6	⁸1	4	2	9
7	2	4	6	5	9	3	1	8
³⁰⁷²2	6	8	⁶1	¹⁹⁴⁴9	4	³⁶⁷⁵7	5	3
4	8	1	3	2	6	9	7	5

©Tetsuya Miyamoto/Gakken

For more information about KenKen™, check out **www.kenken.com**

For more information about KenDoku™, check out **www.ken-doku.com**